NATIONAL GEOGRAPHIC

D0100647

Where Can I Play?

Harley Chan

This is my home.
Where can I play outside?

3

I can play in the yard.

4

This is my home.
Where can I play outside?

I can play on the porch.

This is my home.
Where can I play outside?

I can play in the park.